W9-AWC-400

Mystery history of the
ROMAN
COLOSSEUM

Rhiannon Ash

COPPER BEECH BOOKS
BROOKFIELD, CONNECTICUT

© Aladdin Books Ltd 1997
© U.S. text 1997

Designed and produced by
Aladdin Books Ltd
28 Percy Street
London W1P 0LD

First published in
the United States in 1997 by
Copper Beech Books,
an imprint of
The Millbrook Press
2 Old New Milford Road
Brookfield, Connecticut
06804

Editor
Jim Pipe

Designed by
David West Children's Books
Designer
Simon Morse
Illustrated by
Roger Hutchins
Mike Lacey
Additional illustrations by
David Burroughs
Rob Shone

Printed in Belgium
All rights reserved

Library of Congress
Cataloging-in-Publication Data
Ash, Rhiannon.
Roman colosseum / Rhiannon Ash ;
illustrated by Mike Bell... [et al.].
p. cm. -- (Mystery history of a--)
Includes index.
ISBN 0-7613-0613-7 (lib. bdg.).
-- ISBN 0-7613-0625-0
(trade Hardcover)
1. Colosseum (Rome, Italy)--Juvenile
literature. 2. Amphitheaters--Rome
--Juvenile literature. 3. Rome (Italy)
--Buildings, structures, etc.--Juvenile
literature. I. Title. II. Series: Mystery
history.
DG68.1.F56 1997   97-10020
945'.632--dc21   CIP

Contents

The Roman Colosseum

For 1,900 years, the Colosseum has stood as a symbol of Roman achievement. Originally called the "Flavian amphitheater," the Colosseum was named after the huge, or colossal, statue of Nero that once stood nearby (left).

Today we admire the Romans for their beautiful buildings, well-built roads, and talented writers and artists. But the Colosseum reminds us of their dark side. Here they gathered to watch as millions of animals, thousands of gladiators, and hundreds of innocent Christians (above) were slaughtered to satisfy their lust for blood.

But for the Romans, the Colosseum was a monument to their ruling family, the Flavians, a sacred place where the emperor (below right) greeted his cheering people.

The Mystery of History

We know a great deal about the Romans from ruins such as the town of Pompeii, buried by the volcano Mount Vesuvius in A.D. 79. Roman poets and writers also speak to us through their works. But there's still a lot we don't know. So as you read, try to imagine the sights, sounds, and even smells of Rome. Who knows, your guess might be right. That's the real mystery of history!

You'll find that *Mystery History of the Roman Colosseum* is packed with puzzles and mysteries for you to solve. But before you go any further, read the instructions below to get the most out of the book!

Spot the Plotter

One of the people in this book is plotting to kill the Emperor Domitian! No one knows who, but on page 29 nine suspects have been lined up.

To help you work out who the ringleader of the plot is, clues are given in six Spot the Plotter *boxes (left). If you answer the questions correctly,*

you get clues telling you what the ringleader looks like, e.g. the color of his/her hair. But you'll need to read the book carefully. Happy hunting!

The Emperor's Puzzles

🏆 *The sign of the Emperor's laurel wreath (left) marks a puzzle that is anything from a maze to a math problem. The answers are in The Imperial Answers on each page.*

True or False?

Some pages have a teasing True or False question with an answer (on page 29) that may surprise you!

Hidden History

Try to find the objects cleverly hidden in the picture on each page, then guess if they really belong in ancient Rome!

History Mysteries

Dotted around the pages are questions like: Q3 Do Gladiators have a special diet? *Think about these before reading the answer in The Imperial Answers.*

The Imperial Answers

Answers to Hidden History 🔍 , the History Mysteries Q1 , and the Emperor's Puzzles 🏆 are given in a panel at the bottom of each page.

Survive the Colosseum Game

At the back of the book are full answers to Hidden History and True or False?, a lineup of suspicious-looking Romans (one of whom is plotting to kill Domitian), and, last but not least, a fantastic aerial view of the Colosseum (right) that is full of puzzles!

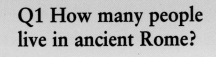
VIA FLAVIA

Q1 How many people live in ancient Rome?

Q2 What language do the Romans speak?

EMPIRE PUZZLE

The Romans are great road builders and sailors, but it still takes a long time to travel around the Empire. Imagine you are inviting friends to the Colosseum opening. If your messages travel 50 miles a day and leave Rome on June 1, will they reach these cities by the end of the month?
a *Lutetia* (Paris, 745mi) **b** *Londinium* (London, 932mi), **c** *Hierosolyma* (Jerusalem, 1,490mi) **d** *Gades* (Cadiz, 1,056mi)?

THE ROMAN EMPIRE

Londinium
Lutetia
Gades
Rome
Hierosolyma
Mediterranean Sea

EMPIRE PUZZLE ANSWER
Yes, just! They'd reach Paris on June 15, London on June 19, Cadiz on June 21, but Jerusalem on June 30!

THE IMPERIAL ANSWERS
Q1 It's difficult to be absolutely certain, but there are probably about one million people living in the city at the time of the Emperor Domitian (A.D. 81–96). The grand total tends to vary. Sometimes disasters kill a lot of the inhabitants, such as the great fire of Rome in A.D. 64. About 54 million people live in the empire, which stretches 2,800 miles from east to west and 2,200 miles from north to south.

Rome, the magnificent capital of the Roman Empire, is even busier than usual. The streets are filled with excited people of all nationalities and ages. Some of them have even made a special journey to the city from the countryside. This is a holiday, and the Roman Emperor Domitian has decided to celebrate by putting on a special show of gladiators for the people. It will take place in a splendid new arena called the Flavian amphitheater. (In later times, this huge structure becomes known as the Colosseum. You can still see its remains in Rome today!)

Q3 When is the Colosseum built?

◎ Hidden History
Can you spot the yo-yo, stamped envelope, road sign, ticket, and roller skates? Which don't belong in a Roman street scene?

Q2 The official language is Latin, though many educated Romans also speak Greek. Slaves and freed men, who originally come from outside Italy, naturally speak their native languages as well as Latin. Rome is probably like most big cities today, where you can hear many different languages being spoken in the streets.
Q3 The Colosseum is started by the Emperor Vespasian, who is Domitian's father, and finished in the year A.D. 80 by the Emperor Titus, Domitian's brother. It was built on the site of a huge palace, which had originally belonged to the disgraced Emperor Nero. The Colosseum can hold an estimated 50,000 people. At the opening ceremony, over 9,000 animals are killed!

Hidden History Answers: The stamp and roller skates don't belong! Turn to page 28 for the reasons why.

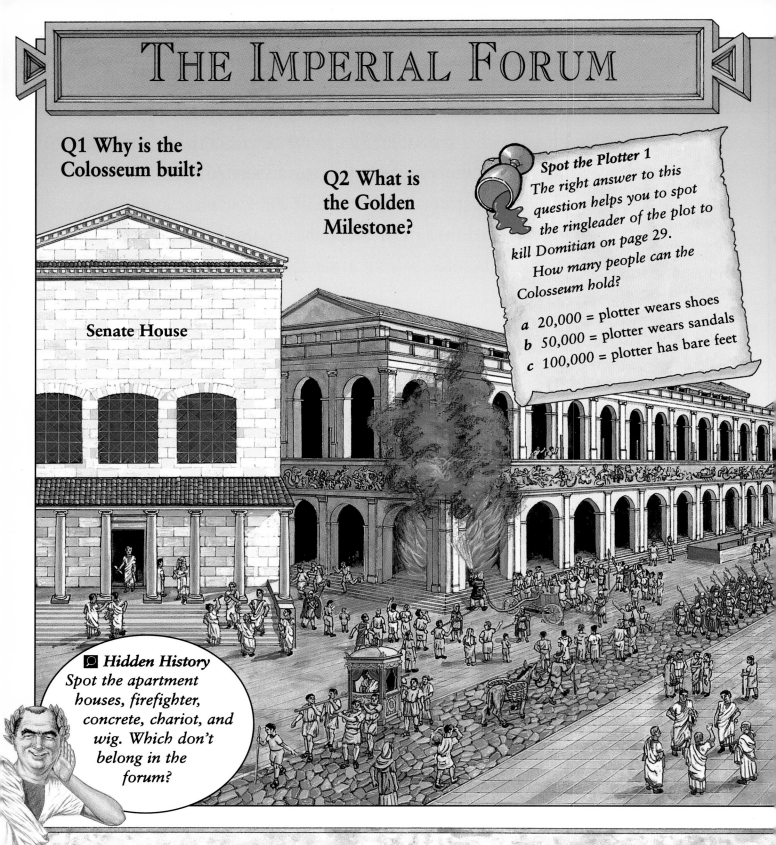

Q1 Why is the Colosseum built?

Q2 What is the Golden Milestone?

Senate House

Spot the Plotter 1
The right answer to this question helps you to spot the ringleader of the plot to kill Domitian on page 29. How many people can the Colosseum hold?

a 20,000 = plotter wears shoes
b 50,000 = plotter wears sandals
c 100,000 = plotter has bare feet

⊙ *Hidden History*
Spot the apartment houses, firefighter, concrete, chariot, and wig. Which don't belong in the forum?

THE IMPERIAL ANSWERS

Q1 To show off! The incredible engineering of the Colosseum reminds ordinary Romans – and the world – of the power of the ruling family. The building measures 187 ft high, 615 ft across at the widest point, and 1,730 ft around the outside. In ancient times, sports festivals are often staged in honor of the gods, so the Colosseum is also a sacred place where watching the games is a partly religious act.

Q2 The Golden Milestone stands in the forum and lists the distances from Rome to the main cities in the Empire. This has some practical value, but mostly, it is to make people in Rome aware that they are living in the greatest city in the world, at the heart of a huge empire.

⊙ *Hidden History Answers: The wig and chariot don't belong! Turn to page 28 for the reasons why.*

The Colosseum is a towering symbol of Rome's power. It stands next to the forum, the heart of life in the empire. Politics, law, religion, and business are all carried out here.

Before the emperors, wealthy men called senators made all the decisions. In Domitian's time, however, real power lies with him. He sets up a big statue of himself in the forum to remind everyone how important he is. The forum also contains temples to gods, such as Saturn, and dead Emperors. Domitian already likes to be called "Master and God!"

True or false? Women can become senators.

COIN PUZZLE

Domitian also shows his power by minting coins that have his picture on them. Two common coins are the silver *denarius* (*right*) and the copper *as* (*bottom*). There are 16 asses to one denarius. Can you work out how much this Roman shopping list costs you in denarii and asses?

- 5 loaves of bread at 3 asses each;
- 9 quails at 6 denarii, 4 asses each;
- 20 amphorae of wine at 4 denarii each;
- 24 oysters at 1 denarius each;
- one pot of *garum* (Roman fish-sauce) at 2 denarii, 2 asses; and
- 20 pears at 6 asses each.

COIN PUZZLE ANSWER

It all adds up to 170 denarii and 13 asses. That's a lot of coins. You might want to take some gold coins with you so you can carry your shopping as well: The gold coin, the aureus, is worth 25 denarii. Archaeologists have found Roman coins in many countries – even China! They are sometimes discovered in gardens where their owners buried them for safekeeping.

Q1 What's going on?

The money for building the Colosseum comes from the emperor's treasuries. These are filled with money from taxes on conquered peoples and the sale of goods from Roman farms. In central Italy, there are many villas like the one shown here. They produce wine, olive oil, wheat, vegetables, and fruit. Most villas are run by a small number of skilled workers. But at harvest time, temporary workers are brought in to help.

The countryside provides for the Colosseum in other ways – aqueducts carry fresh water into the city for the naval battles, and quarries provide the stone for building.

Q2 What's it like living in a villa?

MOSAIC MAZE

Rich people's villas had floors in colored tiles (mosaics). Some were even laid out in maze patterns. Can you get out of this one?

THE IMPERIAL ANSWERS

Q1 It's the harvest. Reaping machines (the very latest devices from Gaul) are being pushed by donkeys to cut the wheat. This is then ground by the mill and stored in large jars in the ground. Slaves in the villa are crushing grapes with their feet to make wine, while in the distance others are farming fish.

Aqueduct

Hidden History
Spot the bees,
wheelbarrow, water-
wheel, pest control, cat,
and sewing machine?
Which don't belong on
a Roman farm?

Spot the Plotter 2
How high is the Colosseum?

a 75 ft = plotter is wearing armor

b 130 ft = plotter wears a cloak

c 187 ft = plotter wears neither armor nor a cloak

Use your clue to work out who the mastermind behind Domitian's death is on page 29.

Q2 As well as being profitable businesses, villas are pleasant places to escape the hustle and bustle of Rome. There are warm baths, centrally heated banqueting rooms, shady courtyards, fountains, and gardens filled with fig trees. The writer Pliny's villa in Tuscany, north Italy, is huge. It has trees cut into the shapes of animals, and a room that has a tree growing inside it. Pliny likes to have his dinner sitting on a marble bench in a shady nook.

Many small villas, however, are just hardworking farms, and the smell of pigs and oxen is never far away!

Hidden History Answers:
Only the sewing machine doesn't belong! For the full reasons why, turn to page 28.

Q1 Why do some tribesmen have beards?

Q2 Are Roman soldiers slaves like gladiators?

THE IMPERIAL ANSWERS

Q1 Amongst the Chatti, a man is not allowed to cut his hair or shave his beard until he has killed his first enemy in battle. So men without beards are more fierce than hairy ones!

Q2 No. At first, Roman citizens have to fight for their country for no money, but around 400 B.C., pay is introduced. It isn't much, but the soldiers can always get extra cash by looting enemy towns after a victory. Long-serving soldiers (who survive!) are given a pension and a plot of land.

Q3 Yes, especially in hot weather, but it's better than getting hit on the head! Legionaries' armor is lighter than that used by gladiators – partly because they also have to carry food and equipment with them.

⊙ *Hidden History Answers: Apart from the gold tooth, none of them belong! See page 28 to find out why.*

Many of the gladiators who fight in the Colosseum are originally captured in battle. There is no shortage of prisoners – the powerful and well-organized Roman army is constantly fighting to defend the empire from hostile tribes from northern Europe and the east.

Here, evening is falling beside the Neckar River in what is now Germany. The year is A.D. 83, and it has been a cold, snowy day. A unit of Roman legionaires has been ambushed by some tough local tribesmen, called the Chatti. But the Romans' superior discipline and weapons help to beat off the attack. They even manage to round up some prisoners, who in a few weeks will find themselves in the slave markets of Rome.

🔍 *Hidden History*
Can you spot the tortoise, machine gun, eagle, gold tooth, and gloves? Which don't belong in a battle between Romans and Chatti?

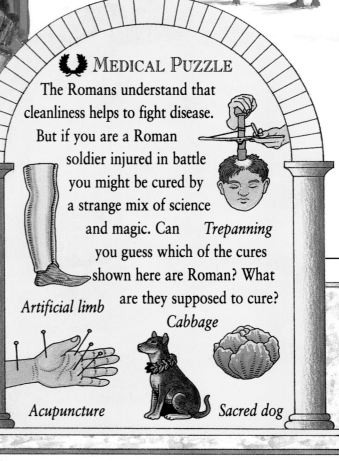

Q3 Isn't it uncomfortable wearing a helmet all day?

MEDICAL PUZZLE

The Romans understand that cleanliness helps to fight disease. But if you are a Roman soldier injured in battle you might be cured by a strange mix of science and magic. Can you guess which of the cures shown here are Roman? What are they supposed to cure?

Trepanning

Artificial limb

Cabbage

Acupuncture

Sacred dog

MEDICAL PUZZLE ANSWER

The Romans use artificial legs to replace those lost in battle. People in the eastern Empire believe that sacred dogs can heal most diseases. Senator Cato (234–149 B.C.) thinks that cabbages soaked in wine cure deafness! Trepanning (removing bone from the skull) is a cure for headaches. But acupuncture (sticking pins into the body) is a Chinese cure for stiff joints or skin diseases.

THE VOYAGE TO ROME

It's a busy day here in Ostia, Rome's seaport. Prisoners of war and wild animals bound for the Colosseum are brought here from the farthest corners of the Empire. Naval captains wait impatiently to unload their cargo after long and often perilous journeys. Once the boats have docked, the crew can relax in the bustling town, which is full of bars and restaurants, and even has a theater. Tomorrow they will complete the 12-mile trip up the Tiber River to Rome.

◎ Hidden History
Spot the rats, lifeboat, windsurfer, semaphore, and lighthouse. Which don't belong in Ostia?

Q1 Do sailors fear pirates or sea monsters?

◎ Hidden History Answers: The rats, windsurfer, and semaphore don't belong! Page 28 has the reasons why.

THE IMPERIAL ANSWERS
Q1 Not much. There have been pirates in the Mediterranean for thousands of years, but the large Roman navy has ruthlessly cleared the waters of the big pirate fleets.

In 78 B.C., for example, the Roman general Julius Caesar is captured by pirates. When they release him after the ransom is paid, he swears to take terrible revenge. He returns and the pirates he does not kill, he crucifies.

Many Roman sailors believe in supernatural monsters like Scylla, who lurks in a cave and seizes passing sailors with her six heads. There are also many sharks in the Mediterranean in Roman times, perhaps even the great white. But storms are the biggest real danger to shipping.

Wheat and barley to feed Rome's inhabitants are also brought here from Egypt and the plains of eastern Europe. Without this supply, Rome would starve. Olive oil, wine, and fruit are also imported, along with exotic goods from distant lands like Africa and China.

Q2 Why is the Tiber River yellow?

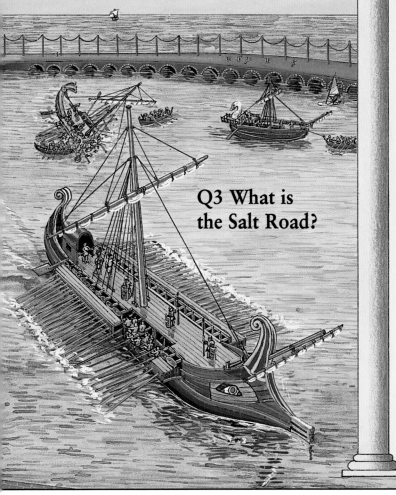

Q3 What is the Salt Road?

⚜ TRADE PUZZLE

The rich citizens of Rome are always looking for new and exciting products. Luckily, the stability of the Roman Empire, known as the *pax romana* ("Roman peace"), means that traders have little to fear as they seek out new items to satisfy their customers.

Goods are transported to Ostia from all over the Empire. The Romans like to boast that you can buy anything from anywhere in the whole world in Rome.

Below you can see some of the items that have recently arrived in the port. Can you guess where they come from?

Pearls

Wheat

Papyrus

Fur

Wild animals

Silk

Spices

Q2 Though Rome's open sewers often drain into the Tiber, the river is tawny yellow because of the mud and silt that flow in its waters. The Roman poets Horace, Virgil, and Ovid all affectionately refer to the "Golden Tiber." Sometimes pictures of the River God even have yellow hair.

Q3 The Salt Road, or *Via Salaria*, is a road running northeast from Rome. Salt is mined at the mouth of the Tiber River and sent to Rome. Merchants use the Salt Road to send their goods around Italy. Since there are no refrigerators, salt is used to preserve meat. Imagine what it tastes like!

⚜ TRADE PUZZLE ANSWER
The wheat and papyrus come mainly from Egypt, the fur from Britain or the region that is now Germany, the wild animals from Africa and India, the silk from China, the spices from Persia and India, and the pearls from India or Britain.

SOLD INTO SLAVERY

Hidden History
Spot the refrigerator, spinning wheel, parrot, handkerchief, and comb? Which don't belong in a Roman slave market?

Q1 Do slaves wear chains?

True or False? The Romans use urine to clean wool.

CLAUDIA AMAT STEFANUM

THE IMPERIAL ANSWERS

Q1 Not usually. Slaves work for their owners, so chains would get in the way. Of course, they could escape,

Hidden History Answers: Only the refrigerator doesn't belong! Turn to page 28 to find out the reasons why.

but there is little point since nobody gives a job to runaway slaves. If they do run away, slaves must avoid the *fugitivarii*, professional slave-catchers who earn a living returning runaway slaves. Today, we may admire Roman civilization, but slaves did many of the dirty jobs that made it possible.

Q2 Of course! Slaves captured in war have their own names, but once they're sold, they usually take a Latin name given by their new master or mistress. They also wear a tablet around their neck with their owner's name and address. Freed slaves often adopt their owner's name.

M en, women, and children are brought to Rome from all over the empire to be sold as slaves. Some are lucky, and are bought by Romans who treat their slaves kindly. If a slave is a skilled scribe, translator, or musician, then the owner is likely to take care of his or her valuable new purchase.

Yet all some slaves have to offer is a pair of strong hands. Manual labor is exhausting without a full belly, and there is always a risk that badly fed slaves will fall ill. But the really unlucky slaves are those that catch the eye of gladiatorial trainers on the lookout for new talent in the slave markets.

Spot the Plotter 3
Where is Ostia?

a *Greece* = plotter has white hair
b *Gaul* = plotter has fair hair
c *Italy* = plotter has brown hair

Use your answer to this question to pick out the leader of the plot to kill Domitian, on page 29.

MARCUS EST PINGUIS

Q2 Do slaves have names?

Q3 Do Roman kids have slaves?

⚜ SLAVE PUZZLE

Roman slaves do all kinds of different jobs. You can see some of the skilled slaves below at work elsewhere in this book. Can you guess what each one does?

Q3 Kind of. Roman kids don't own slaves personally, but rich parents certainly buy their children special slaves to carry their books to school and to make sure that their little darlings don't get into trouble.

⚜ SLAVE ANSWER

a is a barber, on page 15; b is a female gladiator, on page 18; c is a female musician, on page 27; and d is a builder, on page 7. Other slaves are miners, doctors, or work in gangs on farms.

a   b   c   d

SCHOOL FOR GLADIATORS

Some new recruits are being put through their paces here in the gladiator school. They are under the watchful eye of a trainer, named the *lanista*. Many of these future gladiators have been bought in the slave market by buyers who have chosen them especially for their stamina and physique. They receive a general training in handling weapons and fighting an opponent, but they will also learn to specialize.

The gladiators train with wooden weapons and are closely guarded. The Romans are terrified that they will escape and rebel against the empire.

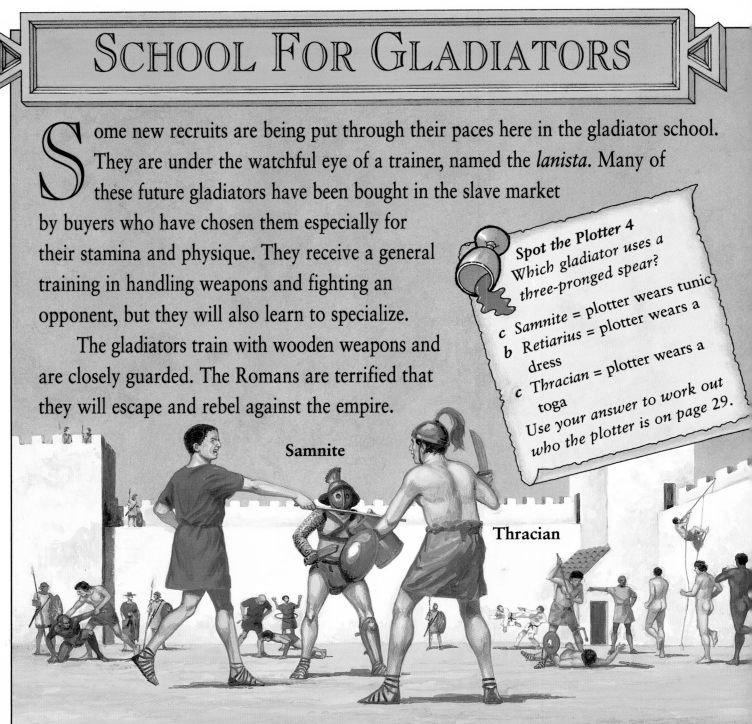

Spot the Plotter 4
Which gladiator uses a three-pronged spear?

c Samnite = plotter wears tunic
b Retiarius = plotter wears a dress
c Thracian = plotter wears a toga

Use your answer to work out who the plotter is on page 29.

Samnite

Thracian

Q1 Why are there different types of gladiators?

Q2 Who is the most famous gladiator in Roman history?

THE IMPERIAL ANSWERS

Q1 To make the fighting more interesting! The lightly-armed fighters move faster, but are more vulnerable. The heavily-armed gladiators are better protected but less nimble. Romans lay bets on contests just as today some people bet on boxing.

Q2 A man named Spartacus, who leads a group of 70 gladiators when they escape from a training school in 73 B.C. They set up a base on Mount Vesuvius, and soon 90,000 runaway slaves from all over Italy have joined them. The rebellious gladiators are only defeated two years later.

Q3 Prisoners of war, slaves, and condemned criminals are the most common types. But rich, young men are also attracted to the thrills and violence of being a gladiator. The Emperor Domitian also puts on a special show where female gladiators fight at night by torchlight.

Q3 Who becomes a gladiator?

Retiarius

Murmillo

◎ *Hidden History*
Spot the chocolate bar, kung fu, stopwatch, hula hoop, and wrestling. Which don't belong in the gladiator training school?

🌿 GLADIATOR PUZZLE

There are four types of gladiators (see *main picture*). The *murmillo* has a fish on the crest of his helmet, the *samnite* wears a visored helmet and carries an oblong shield and a short sword, the lightly armed *retiarius* fights with a net and a trident, and the *thracian* is armed with a round shield and a curved sword named a scimitar.

The four different gladiators have left their equipment in a pile (*below*). What should each pick up, and which type of gladiator is already equipped?

🌿 GLADIATOR ANSWER

Check your answers against the gladiators in the main picture. The gladiator who has already taken his equipment is the murmillo.

◎ *Hidden History Answers: None of them belong! Turn to page 28 to find out the reasons why.*

LET THE GAMES BEGIN

Hidden History
Spot the umbrella, binoculars, cotton candy, water-organ, panda, and rhino. Which belong in the Roman Colosseum?

Q1 Do gladiators always want to kill their opponents?

Q2 Does the emperor decide who lives or dies?

True or false? Children aren't allowed to go to gladiatorial shows.

THE IMPERIAL ANSWERS

Q1 No. Gladiators may live and train together for months before they meet in the arena. It is also expensive to train them, so trainers teach their pupils to wound their opponents. This keeps the audience happy, and the gladiators live to fight another day.

Q2 Yes. However, the emperor pretends to let the audience decide, to show everyone that he listens to his people. Domitian likes the games, but other emperors get bored and fall asleep. This is very unpopular.

Q3 Yes. The day before a contest, gladiators eat lots of meat at a special banquet to give them strength. Before this, they get fat eating barley porridge. This helps to protect them from sword cuts.

Hidden History Answers: The water-organ, umbrella, and rhino belong! See page 28 to find out why.

The games start with a procession of gladiators, dancers, musicians, and priests. Then the gladiators bow to the emperor, shouting, "Hail Caesar! Those who are about to die salute you!" On the day of the games, the maze of corridors below the Colosseum is a hive of activity. As the gladiators fight, animals are hauled up for the next event, and the dead bodies are removed by slaves.

Along with free food supplies, the games are a very important way of keeping Rome's poor happy. The emperor knows that if they go hungry they will riot. Also, in a world without television, the shows are a chance for the emperor to be seen by his people.

Q3 Do gladiators have a special diet?

THRAX
MARCVS

CHARIOT PUZZLE

When the Colosseum is built, the gladiator shows are the Romans' favorite entertainment. But they also enjoy going to the theater and to chariot racing, especially in Rome's huge stadium, the Circus Maximus (*below*).

The word stadium comes from the Roman unit *stadium*. This is divided into 125 *passi* (paces), each 5 ft. If one lap is 1,000 *passi*, and a chariot (*above*) travels at an average speed of 1 *stadium* every 15 seconds, how long does it take to complete a lap?

CHARIOT PUZZLE ANSWER
1,000 passi = 8 stadia, so each lap takes about 8 x 15 seconds = 2 minutes. Most chariot races are run over seven laps. Four teams usually compete – the greens, blues, reds, and whites. The supporters of each team are very passionate. In the 6th century, there is even a riot between rival supporters in Byzantium.

EATEN ALIVE!

Night has fallen and there is a special show in the Colosseum. Some Christians are being fed to the lions in the arena. These people are not criminals, but they have admitted to being Christian. Roman officials think this religion is very sinister, partly because they do not understand it and partly because they do not like any religion or organization that takes power away from them. The most notorious emperor to persecute Christians is Nero, who blames them for the great fire of Rome in A.D. 64.

Q1 How can the Romans tell who is Christian?

🔲 *Hidden History*
Spot the Muslim on his prayer mat, a fish symbol, floodlight, doll, and running shoes. Which might you see in the Roman Colosseum?

Q2 Why do the Romans hate the Christians so much?

THE IMPERIAL ANSWERS

Q1 They can't for sure. People are also accused of being Christian by their enemies, whether it's true or not.

🔲 *Hidden History Answers: Only the fish symbol and doll belong! Turn to page 29 to find out the reasons why.*

Q2 The Romans are actually quite tolerant of most religions. Many worship deities like Egyptian Isis and Persian Mithras as well as their own Roman gods. But Christians believe there is just one god, so there is no room in their religion for the Roman gods. However, Christian ideas appeal to many Romans, especially the poor and slaves. Finally, in A.D. 325, the Emperor Constantine makes Christianity the official religion of the empire. The Emperor Honorius, a Christian, bans gladiator shows in A.D. 404, but wild-beast shows go on for at least another century.

In the past, human and animal sacrifices were a part of ancient Roman religion, and in Domitian's day, animals are still sacrificed as offerings to the Roman gods. Despite this, some Romans are still shocked by the deaths of the Christians.

GODS PUZZLE

The Romans believe that gods and goddesses watch over different areas of their lives. They also have household gods, the *lares* and *penates*, who guard the family home. Can you guess which special areas of life these deities watch over?

Diana   Mercury   Minerva

Neptune   Bacchus   Mars

Q3 Do the Romans believe in ghosts?

Hunt the Assassin 5
Who is Spartacus?

a an emperor = plotter has a helmet or hat

b a pirate = plotter has a beard

c a gladiator = plotter doesn't have a beard, hat, or helmet

Work out the right answer and use your clue to guess who the plotter is on page 29.

Q3 Some do! After the Emperor Caligula is murdered, people believe that his ghost haunts Rome's Lamian gardens until he is properly buried by his sisters. Pliny tells a strange story of a ghost who comes in the middle of the night and cuts people's hair while they are sleeping!

GODS PUZZLE ANSWER

Diana is the goddess of hunting; Mercury is the messenger of the gods; Minerva is goddess of wisdom (with her wise owl); Neptune rules the oceans; Bacchus is the god of drinking and entertainment; and Mars is the god of war.

THE NAVAL BATTLE

Roman audiences at gladiatorial shows always like exciting new spectacles. The rich Romans who pay for the games try interesting ways of matching wild animals like tigers, bears, elephants, and giraffes against humans (see picture on pages 30-31).

When the Colosseum is first opened to the public in A.D. 80, the Emperor Titus has the brilliant idea of filling the arena with water and staging a naval battle. The fighters are condemned criminals, who are dressed up as rival Greek armies – the Corcyreans and Corinthians. Titus even takes the trouble to train horses and bulls so that they can swim, and crocodiles are brought in to finish off drowning gladiators. Even if the fighting is boring, this gives the audience something unusual to look at.

Q1 How is a sea battle staged in the arena?

LIFE AND DEATH

If the audience point their thumbs to their chests (*below*), they want the winner to stab his opponent. If they want the loser to live, they turn their thumbs down, to show the winner to drop his sword (*above*). Some gladiators become famous like sports stars today. Their names are written in graffiti: whose name appears most *below*?

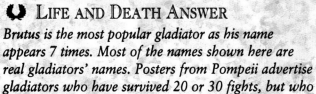

LIFE AND DEATH ANSWER

Brutus is the most popular gladiator as his name appears 7 times. Most of the names shown here are real gladiators' names. Posters from Pompeii advertise gladiators who have survived 20 or 30 fights, but who have only won about half of them – they must be well-liked by the crowd! The Romans write graffiti everywhere. Did you see any on pages 14–15?

Spot the Plotter 6
What is the goddess Minerva linked with?

a *underwear* = plotter is wearing bracelets

b *wisdom* = plotter is wearing earrings

c *birds* = plotter wears neither

Use your answer to discover who the plotter is on page 29.

True or false?
Gladiatorial games are always safe for the audience.

Q2 Why must women sit at the back?

Hidden History
Can you spot the balloons, water wings, zipper, hot dog, and fish. Which don't belong in the Roman Colosseum?

THE IMPERIAL ANSWERS

Q1 No one knows exactly how the water is pumped in. Perhaps the sea battles only take place before the underground corridors are built. The ships in the naval battle are smaller versions of real boats. Having several boats makes the battle more exciting.

Q2 Because Emperor Augustus thinks that they may fall in love with the gladiators! Famous gladiators are like pop stars, and admirers drop flowers on them when they enter the arena.

One *retiarius* (armed with a net and trident) from Pompeii is given the name Crescens, the "netter of girls."

Even the wife of an emperor, Faustina, is said to have a secret love affair with a gladiator: their son, Commodus, becomes the new emperor in A.D. 180.

Hidden History Answers: None of them belong! Turn to page 29 to find out the reasons why.

At The Baths

Q1 How are the baths heated?

Hot room

Cold room

Warm room

Water tank

Furnace

Hidden History
Where's the soap, shower, toothpaste, rubber gloves, *and* library? Which belong in the Roman baths?

Hidden History Answers: Only the toothpaste and library belong in Roman baths! To find out the full reasons why, turn to page 29.

The Imperial Answers

Q1 It is crucial for the warm room, the *tepidarium*, and the hot room, the *caldarium*, to be at the right temperature. So there is a special furnace in which water is heated. This water is then carried through the building in lead pipes so bathers aren't dipping their toes in cold water, unless of course they are in the cold room, the *frigidarium*.

Q2 Some are! The Romans call body odor the "smell of the goat." However, people can always resort to perfumes to hide a bad smell. When a man called Otho invites Emperor ▶

The baths of Titus are right next to the Colosseum, so rich Romans can watch the gladiators and refresh themselves afterward with a relaxing dip. There are public baths all over the Roman Empire, but those in Rome are particularly grand. Baths are not just places where you can get clean. They are more like clubs, where gossip, business, exercise, relaxing massages, and haircuts are all enjoyed!

In fact, rich Romans spend much of their time at leisure, leaving the work to slaves and the poor. Some emperors do not set a good example. They spend their time on entertainment and enjoying wild parties when there is often important business for them to attend to.

Changing room

True or False?
The Emperor Domitian writes a book called "Care of the Hair."

Q2 Are the Romans smelly?

☘ CLOTHES PUZZLE

The Romans wear simple clothes made of wool or linen. The main garment for men and women is the tunic, which hangs to the knees or below. Over this men wear a *toga* and women a *palla*. Both are like large sheets draped around the body.

Below, the attendant at the baths has mixed up the clothing. Which of these clothes belong to what sort of Roman, and which two items aren't Roman at all?

Nero to dinner, he impresses his guest by drenching him in perfume which pours from a gold and silver fountain!

☘ CLOTHES PUZZLE ANSWER
Tunics are worn by almost everyone, boots by soldiers, checked pants by men from Gaul (now France), hats by people who work outside, like farmers, and bikinis by Roman women. Ties and underpants aren't Roman!

THE LAST SUPPER?

The Emperor Domitian is holding a banquet in his luxurious new palace on the Palatine Hill in Rome (*main picture*). His guests recline on couches as they eat, and they are entertained by poets, musicians, and dancers.

However, this lifestyle of baths, banquets, and games does not last forever. German tribes from the north and peoples from the east invade Roman territory many times in the next centuries, and in A.D. 410, Rome is sacked by the Visigoths.

The Colosseum sees its last fight in A.D. 404. Telemachus, a Christian monk, jumps into the arena to protest against the horrors of the games. He is torn apart by a crowd angry at the interruption, but soon after, the Emperor Honorius bans gladitorial shows.

FOOD PUZZLE

The Romans eat all kinds of food that seems strange to us. At an imperial banquet, appetizers are followed by up to seven courses, including a special course such as roast pig stuffed with live birds (*bottom*). For dessert there is fruit, shellfish, snails, and nuts. In the main picture, can you spot the roast heron, stuffed ostrich, champagne, cocktail sausages on sticks, oysters, lobster, grapes, oranges, apples, olives, fish, and roast dormice? Which might you find at a Roman banquet?

FOOD PUZZLE ANSWER

The olives, apples, oranges, grapes, sausages, and fish you might find on many Roman dinner tables. But the lobster, the roast dormice, roast heron, stuffed ostrich, and oysters are special delicacies that only the rich can afford. The Romans love wine, but sparkling wines like champagne are first developed in the Middle Ages.

Hidden History
Spot the skeleton, toilet paper, toaster, corkscrew, and fork. Which don't belong at a Roman banquet?

Q1 Are Domitian's parties always fun?

Q2 Is Domitian a bit strange?

Q3 Why does Domitian's palace have corridors lined with polished marble?

Q1 No! On one occasion, Domitian invites some senators to a banquet. The food, attendants' clothes, plates, glasses, and even the room are all black, and the place names are carved like tombstones. The senators are terrified that Domitian is out to kill them, but he just wants to scare them!

Q2 Not compared with the Emperor Caligula (A.D. 37–41), who thinks he's a god and makes his horse a senator.
Perhaps the oddest Emperor is Elagabalus (A.D. 218–222), who once showers his guests with so many rose petals they suffocate. He also hides spiders and lions' dung in the food!

Q3 Because he's terrified of being assassinated and wants to see if he's being followed. He's quite right to be scared: In A.D. 96 he's stabbed to death.

Hidden History Answers: None of them belong, apart from the skeleton! See page 29 to find out why.

A Hoard Of Answers

Pages 4–5
Roman kids had toys such as tops, swings, see-saws, and *yo-yos*. The first emperor, Augustus (31 B.C.–A.D. 14), introduced a mail system for official business in the empire, but the first *stamp* was used in Britain in 1840. *Road signs* existed in Roman times. Without a clay or bone token, used like *tickets*, you couldn't enter the Colosseum. *Roller skates* were first made by Belgian Joseph Merlin in 1760.

Pages 6–7
Poor people lived in *apartment houses* all over Rome. Called *insulae*, they were cold and often caught fire. During the famous fire of A.D. 64, the Emperor Nero is supposed to have played his lyre while Rome burned. Augustus was the first emperor to organize brigades of *firefighters* for Rome (but without today's helmets and safety gear). Roman builders tended to use whatever they could, but they did use a kind of *concrete*, which gained its strength from volcanic ash. Some Romans wore wigs, but not magistrates (*judges*) as judges in Britain do today. The Romans had *chariots*, but as they were banned from Rome's center during the daytime you wouldn't see any in the forum.

Pages 8–9
Bees were kept by Romans everywhere as honey was important in Roman cooking as a sweetener, and was even used to treat coughs and ulcers. Roman poets said that honey fell on flowers from heaven for bees to gather. The *wheelbarrow* and *waterwheel* were common in Roman farms. The writer Pliny mentions Roman *pest control*, such as soaking seeds in poison to protect against insects. *Cats* were brought to Italy from Egypt, but Romans originally trained ferrets to catch mice! The first *sewing machine* was made in 1846 by American Elias Howe.

Pages 10–11
Any self-respecting *tortoise* hibernates in winter, but you might have seen the Roman "tortoise" formation on a battlefield (*left*). Likewise, though Roman armies did not have a real *eagle*, each legion was led by a symbolic eagle carried on a pole (*bottom*). The Romans did not have *machine guns*, but they did face some amazing quick-firing catapults fighting against the Greeks (*below left*)! The Romans did not have *gloves*, but some tunics had long sleeves, called *manicae*, which covered their hands. Each hand was put in the sleeve opposite to keep it warm. Roman dentists learned from the Etruscans of central Italy, who from 700 B.C. were producing well-fitting *gold teeth*.

Pages 12–13
Rats didn't arrive in Europe until the 11th century, but mice were certainly a problem in the granaries at Ostia. *Windsurfing* is a modern craze, though Roman children did play on little chariots that were driven by the wind. The Romans used fire signals instead of flags for *semaphore* (communicating over long distances). *Lighthouses* are as old as shipping. Claudius' lighthouse at Ostia was well-known. *Lifeboats* were not used as widely as today, but the Romans did have them.

Pages 14–15
Romans kept food cold with ice (*above right*) or stored it in a cool cellar, but there were no *refrigerators*. Romans who wove cloth for a living had complicated mechanical looms, but there were also simple *spinning wheels* for household use. *Parrots* were kept as pets by rich Romans – they even wrote poems about them. The

Romans had *handkerchiefs* and *combs*. One poet wrote how his girlfriend's hair fell out because she had dyed it too often.

Pages 16–17
The first *chocolate* was drunk, by the Mayas of central America from A.D. 100. *Kung fu* is a Chinese martial art unknown to the Romans. The *stopwatch* had not been invented in Roman times, but they used sand timers to time races. The *hula hoop* was only invented in 1958 by Americans Richard P. Knerr and Arthur K. "Spud" Melvin, though Roman children did play with hoops (see page 9). *Wrestling* was a big sport in Roman times, but gladiators preferred to use weapons.

Pages 18–19
Romans carried *umbrellas* to protect against the hot summer sun, but there was also a huge canopy in the Colosseum, the *velarium*, that was hauled out by sailors (see *pages 30-31*). The Romans didn't have *binoculars*, but Pliny refers to the Emperor Nero watching the games through a kind of emerald. *Cotton candy* is made from sugar, which the Romans didn't have. The Romans had *water-organs*, which were played during the games (see *page 29, center*). The *panda* is a gentle Chinese animal and was never brought to fight in the arena, but the Romans did bring the *rhino* to Rome.

Spot the Plotter
Now's the time to use your six clues to pick out the leader of the plot against the Emperor Domitian. Perhaps you saw one of the people in the lineup (right) acting suspiciously in the book? If you can't tell who the guilty person is from your clues, some of your answers must have been wrong. The answer is on page 32!

Pages 20–21

Islam, the religion practiced by *Muslims*, was founded by the Arabian prophet Muhammad in the 7th century A.D., and so did not exist in Roman times. The *fish on the wall* was one of the first symbols of the early Christians. The Colosseum was lit in the evening by hundreds of torches – there was no electricity for *floodlights*. Roman children had *dolls* to play with. Modern *running shoes* were developed by German Adi Dassler (Adidas) in 1920. Roman athletes usually ran in their bare feet.

Pages 22–23

Rubber *balloons* are a 20th-century invention as are *water wings*, though Assyrian soldiers inflated pigs' stomachs to help them float across rivers as early as the 8th century B.C. (*above right*). The *zipper* was invented by American Whitcomb L. Judson in 1893. The Romans fastened their clothes together with special pins. The *hot dog* did not exist as a snack in Roman times, though Romans could buy sausages from the butcher. *Fish* were not part of the spectacle of the naval battle, but *murmillo* gladiators did have a fish crest on their helmets.

Pages 24–25

Instead of using *soap*, the Romans covered themselves in oil and scraped it off with a special stick called a *strigil*. *Showers* were built by the ancient Greeks in the 4th century B.C., but the Romans preferred baths. The Romans used toothpicks to clean their teeth, and an early form of *toothpaste* made from the ashes of dogs' teeth mixed with honey. The poet Ovid wrote that people with bad teeth should keep their mouths shut! The first *rubber clothes* were made by the peoples of central America in the 13th century A.D. As a trip to the baths could involve hours of discussion, most had a *library* to settle arguments about poems, history, or literature.

Pages 26–27

At Roman banquets, there were often models of *skeletons,* some of them full-sized. They were there to remind the guests to enjoy life, because death could catch up with them at any moment. *Toasters* did not exist in Roman times because there was no electricity. Wine was stored in large tapered earthenware jars called *amphorae*, so the Romans did not need *corkscrews*. In Domitian's day Romans ate with their fingers or with spoons, but *forks* were used in the Eastern Roman Empire in the 4th century A.D. Instead of *toilet paper*, the Romans used a stick with a sponge on the end (*above right*).

TRUE OR FALSE?

Page 7 *False* – Senators were always men. There were some powerful women in Roman politics, such as Augustus' wife Livia, but they were unusual.

Page 14 *True* – In Rome, big urinals stood on street corners. Clothmakers took the contents to clean their fleeces, which they then made into wool. When the Emperor Vespasian taxed these urinals, they were named after him as a joke!

Page 18 *False* – Children went to the gory shows, but they didn't always enjoy them. The Emperor Caracalla went as a child to a gladiatorial show, but cried and turned his eyes away from the arena.

Page 23 *False* – Sometimes badly built amphitheaters collapsed, as at Fidenae, or there could be riots. Two towns, Pompeii and Nuceria, were banned from putting on shows for ten years after violent clashes between rival supporters.

Page 25 *True* – Domitian was bald, but he still wrote "Care of the Hair" and wore a wig when he was shown on coins.

Survive the Colosseum Game
Once you've picked out the leader of the plot from the lineup, play the game on pages 30–31.

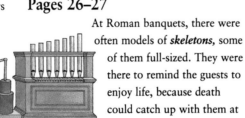

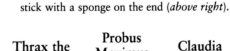

| Senator Cassius | Marcus the Slave | Domitian's wife Domitia | Thrax the gladiator | Probus Maximus | Claudia Flavia | Drusus Civilis | Livia Porcus | General Agrippa |

INTRODUCTION

The scene here shows the Colosseum packed with Romans lusting for blood. The giant canopy has been pulled out to protect them from the sun, and gladiators are fighting wild beasts in the arena.

Imagine you are a gladiator. Try the puzzles and see if you can survive the tough training and the horrors of the wild beast show before escaping from the arena. Good luck – the answers are at the bottom of page 31!

1 ANIMAL TRACKER

If you're going to have to fight against wild animals, it's worth knowing their tracks so you can tell what's hiding around the corner. Which tracks *below* should tell you to watch out?

a   b   c
d   e   f

7 TIME TO ESCAPE!

Now you've worked out the secret message, can you escape from the maze of corridors beneath the Colosseum? Be quick, because the *fugitivarii* (slave catchers) will soon be after you!

6 MIRROR MESSAGE

Safely beneath the arena, you find this message telling you how to escape the maze of tunnels (*left*). Using a mirror, write down these instructions:

To escape, you must avoid the spring and the will animals. But once you get a swords from the center of the maze, you can fight past the lion and escape.

XI

VIII

2 SPOT THE DIFFERENCE

When you're fighting as a gladiator, it helps to have the best equipment possible. There's nothing worse than a shield breaking when a tiger wants you for dinner. Look at the four shields *below* – which one is missing a piece?

a

b

c

d

3 THINK FAST

See how fast you can get from A to B in the order triangle–circle–square–triangle–circle–square and so on, hopping in any direction. Then go back to A following blue–red–green–blue–red–green, etc.

A

B

XIV

XII

4 HAPPY BIRTHDAY?

The Roman calendar is based on special days known as the Kalends (1st), Nones (5th), and Ides (13th) of most months. From these three points, the date is calculated as the number of days before a special day (including that day). For example, if your birthday is January 2, you are born four days before the Nones.

As a gladiator, you would hope to fight on the emperor's birthday as he is more likely to be in a good mood and will let you live if you are defeated.

If the emperor's birthday is three days before the Ides of April, what day is it in the modern calendar?

5 GATE NUMBER

You've made it into the Colosseum – and there are wild animals everywhere. But a friend has told you that one gate leads to safety. However, the gates are numbered with Roman numerals. The Roman counting system is as follows:

1 = I, 2 = II, 3 = III, 4 = IV, 5 = V
6 = VI, 7 = VII, 8 = VIII, 9 = IX, 10 = X

Look at the gates in the main picture. You know that only a gate with an odd number is safe to enter. Which is it, and can you guess what the number is?

ANSWERS 1 *a = bull, b = horse, c = lion, d = ostrich, e = elephant, f = bear, so you need to watch out for all of them, apart from tracks b and d.* **2** *Shield c is the odd one out – it has a piece missing from the knob in the center of the shield.* **3** *How long did it take to get from A to B and back? Any turns under a minute are pretty amazing.* **4** *The emperor's birthday is April 11.* **5** *The odd number is XI = 11.* **7** *Once you've picked up some armor from the middle, the way out of the maze is past the lion on the right.*

INDEX

Spot the Plotter Answer

Gasp! It was Domitian's wife Domitia who was behind his assassination all along. Did you spot her handing a dagger to a slave on page 27? A small group of senators also in the plot chose a noble, Nerva, as the new emperor before they had Domitian killed in A.D. 96.